Buried with Christ

Understanding Baptism

SCOTT FRANKS

ISBN: **1484076931**
ISBN-13: **978-1484076934**

DEDICATION

To my parents, who prayed for me every day before and after I was baptized, and to every other parent doing the same for their kids.

CONTENTS

FIRST, A WORD TO PARENTS

If you are reading this as a parent who will be discussing baptism with your child, I just want you to know I have been there, too. I actually had one daughter surprise me with a PowerPoint presentation about why she wanted to be baptized. I know the trepidation when you have a kid who seems too young yet is miserable because she is not baptized. I also know the concern when a kid appears ready to you, and yet is not mentioning baptism at all.

I just want to give you a little perspective that will hopefully bring some clarity and peace. Remember: You are the parent, and it's okay to tell your child he/she is not ready to be baptized.

God made you the parent of this child for a reason. We parents are there to lead and guide and shape our children, and the process is rarely simple and never perfect. Sometimes we dangle a carrot, sometimes we set up guardrails, sometimes we strike bargains, and sometimes we just have to say no.

Just like with getting a cell phone or a driver's license or going to summer camp, baptism is a decision in which we rightfully play a part, and especially for younger children, we have a right to say "not yet."

This book is intended to help you with that conversation, and hopefully as you go through it with your child, it will give you more confidence in deciding if and when he/she is ready for this momentous commitment.

But I know that doesn't address a lingering fear for some of you: What if I tell my child to wait and then he/she never gets baptized? That's the real fear, isn't it? I'll give you two answers, one short, one much longer.

The short answer is, if you told your eight-year-old that she was not ready to be baptized, and now she is thirteen and still not baptized, then she wasn't ready when she was eight. I really believe that.

Becoming a disciple is a process. I don't believe we are dealing with one brief window in which all the stars align and we must get that kid dunked or else. I think we too often give in to a momentary swell of emotion, or a child's desire to be like her friends, or simple curiosity. This is a matter of her heart, but also her ability to comprehend the commitment she is making. She may have the desire, but not yet the maturity, to make this decision.

If you don't think your child is ready, then praise that desire within her that wants to follow Christ, but tell her you want her to wait a while. Hopefully, this book will help you articulate your reasoning. If the desire is real, she'll bring it up again. If time passes to the place where you think she is ready, but she is not talking about it anymore, then you can certainly initiate the conversation.

I really don't believe that we have just one chance to get this right, and if we exercise our parental judgment and delay a child, then we may make a mistake with eternally permanent consequences. I just don't think it works that way. And that leads to my second, much longer answer.

We've all heard the one verse pulled out in every sermon on parenting: **Proverbs 22:6,** *"Train up a child in the way he should go, and when he is old, he will not stray from it."*

Some of you think, well if that is true, then you must have done something wrong because your 23-year-old is unbaptized and no longer in church. Listen, this verse is not a guarantee. It is true in the sense that it is always the best approach to parenting, but it is not always foolproof.

I know that because the Bible itself proves that. The Bible gives us plenty of examples of good parents producing rebellious kids, and wicked parents producing righteous kids. Ahaz was an extremely evil king in Judah, yet his son Hezekiah was zealous and righteous, yet Hezekiah's son Manasseh immediately resumed the wicked practices of his grandfather. There is no explanation in that section of scripture for how someone like Hezekiah could turn out so good, or how Manasseh turned out so bad.

Now there is no doubt that our behaviors and actions as parents can have great influence on our kids, and sometimes our kids pay for our mistakes. That is exactly what God warned when giving the Ten Commandments:

Exodus 20:5b – 6 (ESV) *". . . for I the LORD your God am a Jealous God, visiting the iniquity of the fathers on the children to the third and the fourth generation of those who hate me, but showing steadfast love to thousands of those who love me and keep my commandments."*

God is jealous because He wants us to know Him, live in Him, obey Him for our own good. Because of that, He may allow the negative consequences of a parent's sin to impact children or grandchildren, but for the purpose of turning those kids back to God because God is jealous for them too. God wants them to know Him too.

So yes, there are consequences to the mistakes we make as parents, but God also said this in the Mosaic Law: **Deuteronomy 24:16 (HCSB)** *Fathers are not to be put to death for their children or children for their fathers; each person will be put to death for his own sin.*

God told the Israelites they were not to punish parents for what their children did, and children were not to be punished for what their parents had done. You know what that tells me? That tells me that even if a parent does everything right, their children may still fall away from God, and God doesn't blame the parent for that.

When it comes to how God will treat our kids, when it comes to how God will judge us and our kids, God does not shut the door on a child because of what a parent did or did not do. God does not punish us because of what our parents did or did not do. Yes, there may be negative consequences for what parents did, but that is not the same as God punishing us for what our parents did.

I want to show you something in Ezekiel 18. The Israelites saw that warning back in the Ten Commandments about how God will visit the iniquity of the fathers on the third and fourth generation, so they assumed that if something bad happened to them, it was God punishing them for what their parents had done. They even had a saying: "The fathers eat sour grapes, and the children's teeth are set on edge." In other words, if parents make mistakes, God will make their kids pay for it. They thought that their parents had messed up their relationship with God, and that's why things were not going well for them now with God.

I want you to listen to what God says about that in **Ezekiel 18:1-20 (NIV):**

The word of the Lord came to me: [2] *"What do you people mean by quoting this proverb about the land of Israel: 'The parents eat sour grapes, and the children's teeth are set on edge'?*

"As surely as I live, declares the Sovereign Lord, you will no longer quote this proverb in Israel. For everyone belongs to me, the parent as well as the child—both alike belong to me. The one who sins is the one who will die.

[5] *"Suppose there is a righteous man who does what is just and right.* [6] *He does not eat at the mountain shrines or look to the idols of Israel. He does not defile his neighbor's wife* [7] *He does not oppress anyone, but returns what he took in pledge for a loan. He does not commit robbery but gives his food to the hungry and provides clothing for the naked.* [8] *He does not lend to them at interest or take a profit from them.*

He withholds his hand from doing wrong and judges fairly between two parties. [9] *He follows my decrees and faithfully keeps my laws. That man is righteous; he will surely live, declares the Sovereign Lord.*

[10] *"Suppose he has a violent son, who sheds blood or does any of these other things* [11] *(though the father has done none of them): "He eats at the mountain shrines. He defiles his neighbor's wife.* [12] *He oppresses the poor and needy. He commits robbery. He does not return what he took in pledge. He looks to the idols. He does detestable things.* [13] *He lends at interest and takes a profit.*

Will such a man live? He will not! Because he has done all these detestable things, he is to be put to death; his blood will be on his own head.

[14] *"But suppose this son has a son who sees all the sins his father commits, and though he sees them, he does not do such things:* [15] *"He does not eat at the mountain shrines or look to the idols of Israel. He does not defile his neighbor's wife.* [16] *He does not oppress anyone . . . He keeps my laws and follows my decrees.*

He will not die for his father's sin; he will surely live. [18] *But his father will die for his own sin, because he practiced extortion, robbed his brother and did what was wrong among his people.*

[20] *The one who sins is the one who will die. The child will not share the guilt of the parent, nor will the parent share the guilt of the child. The righteousness of the righteous will be credited to them, and the wickedness of the wicked will be charged against them.*

So God does not punish our kids for our mistakes in a soul-damaging way. God does not hold a grudge against them on Judgment Day because of what we did. God does not somehow add on to our mistakes to make it more difficult for our kids to stay faithful to Him.

But I know that some of you worry that you pushed too hard, or you didn't push hard enough, or you wish you could take back that time you overreacted. You wonder if you were too strict, or not strict enough. You keep replaying the tape, searching for the reason why your kids never got baptized or have fallen away from church.

Maybe they are teenagers or even young adults now and you don't know if they will ever get right with God. I'm sorry that I don't have a sure-fire solution to fix that, but I do have a truth to give you.

Before I tell you that truth, I will say this. If you feel there is something you need to say to your kids about their spiritual state, then say it. If you think you need to apologize to them for something you did, then apologize. Continue to pray for them. If they have strayed, pray that they will continually encounter those intersections where they see clearly where their current path is leading them. Continually pray that they will encounter influences that encourage them to try again the path that leads to God. Continue to love them the way God loves you, and continue to model to them the life you want them to live in Christ.

Now here is that truth: Ultimately, even a kid raised by dedicated Christian parents, heavily involved in a good church with a dynamic, caring youth minister, sent to a private Christian school ever since kindergarten, even that kid will encounter numerous intersections in life where he has to decide for himself if he will follow God. And since it is a choice, he may choose not to.

Our kids' real Father is not going to force them to love Him, obey Him, or come to Him. We can't force them to do that either. It remains and must be their choice.

Don't misunderstand me. I'm not advocating a hands-off approach to spiritual parenting. Just the opposite. As a parent, I'll do everything I can, but I can't do everything.

At some point they have to decide if they want a relationship with their Heavenly Father, and if they do, then they will find Him, maybe because of our parenting, maybe despite our parenting.

2 Chronicles 15:2 (ESV) *The Lord is with you while you are with Him. If you seek Him, He will be found by you . . ."*

That's David talking to his son Solomon, telling him that now, son, you have a choice to make about your relationship with God. God wants to be found. God the good Father is just waiting for each and every person – He is right there, waiting for us -- but it is up to us to seek Him.

Isaiah 65:1 (ESV)
I was ready to be sought by those who did not ask for me;
I was ready to be found by those who did not seek me.
I said, "Here I am, here I am," to a nation that was not called by my name.

Even the people who never seek God out, God is yearning even for them. He is not hiding from anyone. He wants to be sought and found.

In the story of the prodigal son, it was the prodigal who had to decide to come home. The father – God – eagerly waited for him, and once the prodigal made the decision to return, ran to meet him, but it was the prodigal who ultimately had to decide what his relationship with God would be.

God knows our hearts and the hearts of our children. He is aware of what each of us could and could not do, of what we know and don't at any given time. He is the loving Father who is ready to be sought, who wants to be found, who does not hide from someone seeking Him, and He is the one who ultimately judges us. When our holy God judges us, we can be assured He judges us rightly.

I find great comfort in that, because the question of when a child is ready to be baptized is such an individual, subjective decision. We can trust in His grace, and just prayerfully do our best to honor Him as we discuss this with our kids.

THE AGE OF ACCOUNTABILITY

Before we get into the actual lessons, I want to share something else with you parents that again may help you in making decisions about the readiness of your child for baptism. If you grew up in church like I did, then you are familiar with the idea of the age of accountability. Even if you didn't, the idea is not unique to just Christians.

In legal terms, our society has set ages by which someone should be able to "own" their decisions and be held accountable for commitments they make. By 15 or 16, we think kids are responsible enough to drive a car, but not old enough to make a life-long commitment like marriage. We trust them with important decisions like voting at age 18, but make them wait until 21 to buy alcohol.

Those age limits are somewhat arbitrary. We all know 16-year-olds that have no business behind the wheel of a car, and 30-year-olds that are still too selfishly immature to get married or be parents.

I've heard the concept of accountability compared to a dimmer knob on a chandelier. As with so many things in life, it is rarely the case that suddenly we are ready or fully competent. It is not like we go to bed one night immature and wake up the next morning as mature adults. Maturity and accountability do not work like a light switch that snaps from "off" to "on."

Instead, it is like a dimmer knob, and the transition from dark to light is gradual. We mature in stages over time, and that process is uneven and happens at different speeds for each of us. Perhaps that is why, in its wisdom, the Bible does not specify an age at which people *must* be baptized because they are accountable to God and will be condemned if they are not baptized. An age of accountability is simply not in scripture.

In the Jewish faith, the age of accountability is thirteen for boys and twelve for girls, but that is a rather modern development and not something from the Bible. A man in biblical times was expected to reach thirty years of age before he could speak with authority as a rabbi or teacher for others, but authority is not the same as accountability.

It is worth noting that the age of twenty was a significant milestone for accountability in the Old Testament. Once an Israelite reached twenty-years-old, he had to pay the "atonement money" of a half shekel contribution towards the service of the tabernacle (Exodus 30:14). At twenty, the men were considered of age to fight in war (Numbers 1:3). At age twenty, Levites could begin their service in the temple (Ezra 3:8).

Perhaps most applicable to our discussion is how God used the age of twenty when holding the Israelites accountable for rebellion against Him. If you remember the story of the Exodus, the Israelites were freed from slavery in Egypt, led by Moses through the Sinai peninsula, and then headed north to claim the Promised Land. Moses sent twelve spies to scout out that land, but ten of them came back and reported that it would be impossible for them to conquer the great, fortified cities of Canaan. On hearing this, the people lost heart and even talked about killing Moses and returning to Egypt. They were convinced that they would be defeated and their children killed or enslaved by the pagan Canaanites.

Because of their rebellious lack of faith, God condemned them to wander in the wilderness for forty years, until that generation had died off and a new generation had been raised willing to faithfully follow God into the Promised Land.

I want you to notice the age cut-off for that judgment:

Numbers 14:29-31 (ESV)
. . . your dead bodies shall fall in this wilderness, and of all your number, listed in the census from twenty years old and upward, who have grumbled against me, not one shall come into the land where I swore that I would make you dwell, except Caleb the son of Jephummeh and Joshua the son of Nun. But your little ones, who you said would become a prey, I will bring in, and they shall know the land that you have rejected.

In other words, God held accountable all the Israelites twenty years old and up, but those under twenty He did not judge as punishable. It is even more interesting to see the words used in Deuteronomy, when Moses retells this event:

Deuteronomy 1:39 (ESV)
And as for your little ones, who you said would become a prey, and your children, who today have no knowledge of good and evil, they shall go in there. And to them I will give it, and they shall possess it.

Arguably, even the nineteen-year-olds were lumped into the category of children with no knowledge of good and evil. Well obviously a nineteen-year-old knows right from wrong. This is not talking about knowing right from wrong, but reaching a level of maturity for which they would be held accountable by God.

The only other place that phrase – "knowledge of good and evil" – is found verbatim in the Bible is back in Genesis, in the Garden of Eden, where Adam and Eve willfully experienced the forbidden tree of the knowledge of good and evil. They did so fully knowing what God had said were the consequences: they would surely die.

I'm not suggesting that we all are accountable before God at age twenty, but these verses do say that in terms of being judged for our choices spiritually, that does not happen when we know right from wrong (which could be in the toddler years), but at a later stage of maturity when we comprehend the true nature of sin and our behavior reflects that comprehension. That is something we will talk about more in the next chapter.

As far as the New Testament, there is no "age of accountability" mentioned there either, but it gives no specific examples of children being baptized. Every individual baptism account in the book of Acts involves an adult.

It is true that when Peter preaches baptism in Acts 2, he mentions children:

Acts 2:38-39 (NIV)
[38] Peter replied, "Repent and be baptized, every one of you, in the name of Jesus Christ for the forgiveness of your sins. And you will receive the gift of the Holy Spirit. [39] The promise is for you and your children and for all who are far off—for all whom the Lord our God will call."

In context, though, Peter is emphasizing how the promise of forgiveness and salvation will extend beyond just the Jews gathered that day in Jerusalem, on to future generations and other, Gentile nations.

Later in Acts, there is the story of the Philippian jailer, and it mentions that his whole family or household was also baptized:

Acts 16:33 (NIV)
[33] *At that hour of the night the jailer took them and washed their wounds; then immediately he and all his household were baptized.*

That is all we are told. Yes, it is possible kids were part of that, but we don't know their ages. It would not be wise to make too many assumptions from that one verse.

So we are not given a story of a child being baptized, and we are not given an age by which someone should be baptized. What we are left with are scriptures that describe the doctrinal, spiritual, and practical implications of baptism.

If we don't have a minimum age of accountability, what standards should we use?

I would suggest that the time is not right until a few things are evident:

- Does a child understand the essential truths about sin and salvation?
- Is he/she motivated for the right reasons?
- Does he/she have the maturity to make and own the commitment represented by baptism?

I'll be the first to admit my three standards are not given in any sort of list in the Bible. For that matter, the old five steps of salvation that so many of us learned (hear, believe, confess, repent, be baptized) are not given in any neat package in scripture either. Those were used as a teaching tool because they corresponded to five fingers on a hand. The process of belief and salvation and discipleship is never so neat or linear, in scripture or life.

In the rest of this book, we will look at what scripture says about salvation and baptism and discipleship, and hopefully in synthesizing all of those teachings, you will be equipped to assess if your child is ready to be baptized.

I hope that you express your pride in your children for thinking about baptism. They are asking some of the most important questions of their lives. They are thinking about the stuff that really matters. I hope you also assure them that even if they are not yet baptized, they still count in God's eyes, and their faith is real and valid.

Listen to what Jesus says about kids in **Mark 10:13-16 (ESV):**
[13] And they were bringing children to him that he might touch them, and the disciples rebuked them. [14] But when Jesus saw it, he was indignant and said to them, "Let the children come to me; do not hinder them, for to such belongs the kingdom of God. [15] Truly, I say to you, whoever does not receive the kingdom of God like a child shall not enter it." [16] And he took them in his arms and blessed them, laying his hands on them.

Jesus holds up kids as an example of the sort of faith we all should have. Kids can make a difference for God's kingdom and show Christ to others in all sorts of ways even before they are baptized. Now baptism will be necessary at some point, but they may not be ready to make that commitment yet, and that is okay.

This is a process, a relationship that will last their whole lives. Baptism is one step in that process, and you want to make sure they are ready because it is important and forever and will require a lot of them.

I explain the spiritual relationship between unbaptized children and God by comparing it to a different sort of relationship: marriage. My wife's name is Sheree. After going on just one date with her, I knew I liked her. As it turns out, I never went out on a date with any other girl after my first date with Sheree. I never kissed another girl after my first date with Sheree. But it would not have been appropriate for me, on that first date, to tell her "I want to be with you forever – let's get married!" Before I made that commitment to her, I needed to get to know her better, and honestly, get to know myself better.

I liked Sheree from the beginning, and it turns out I have belonged to her since we first met, but committing to live with her the rest of my life needed to happen at the right time. It works that way in our relationship with Jesus, too. Some part of your children already knows about him, and they know they like him and want to follow him. But even if they feel that way in their hearts, there may be some other things that they need to know and experience before they are ready to make a life-long commitment like baptism.

The first of these, I think, is knowing the true nature of sin. That's where we'll start in lesson #1.

#1 THE TRUTH ABOUT SIN
It is worse than you think

<u>Discussion Question:</u> What are your earliest memories of knowing right and wrong, yet still choosing to do what was wrong or forbidden anyway? Why do we make choices like that?

<u>Discussion Question:</u> How would you define sin?

- A good short answer to that question is found in **James 4:17** (NIV): *[17] If anyone, then, knows the good they ought to do and doesn't do it, it is sin for them.*
- But the truth about the nature of sin goes beyond that. Sin is rebellion. We have rebellion in our human hearts. Lying and manipulation come pretty naturally to most of us, even as little kids. We disobey and lie, even as toddlers. We have all done something even though we knew it was wrong, and when we do that, we may be rebelling against our parents or against a teacher, but in the end, all sin is rebellion against God.

Sin is actually probably worse than we think in God's eyes. At least that seems to be the point in the story of Adam and Eve. We'll look at that story next to get a better understanding of sin and what it does to us.

It all started with one lie: "You will not surely die."

God created Eden, the perfect home for Adam and Eve, and in Eden He gave them everything they needed. Everything was there for them to enjoy, except for one forbidden tree, one place they could not go: the tree of the knowledge of good and evil. If they "knew" or experienced the evil represented by that tree, God told them they would surely die (Genesis 2:15-17). That tree represented rebellion against God, and God told them to stay away from it for their own good. If they ate from that tree, it meant that they didn't trust what God told them.

But Satan, the serpent, convinced them they would not surely die and that God must be hiding something. Satan convinced Eve there must be something more than what God was giving her, and she should be able to experience it. The cruel thing was Satan knew that if she listened to him, she would surely die.

John 8:44 (NIV1984) [44]*. . . [The Devil] was a murderer from the beginning, not holding to the truth, for there is no truth in him. When he lies, he speaks his native language, for he is a liar and the father of lies.*

Satan lied to Eve knowing it would kill her. Why? Because Satan hates people. He has nothing to offer us and can do nothing for us that doesn't end in disappointment and damage and death. So Satan lies to us about sin. The truth is that when we sin, it breaks something inside us and it breaks something between us and God.

Discussion Question: Have you ever broken something that you couldn't fix or pay for? What did you do?

Genesis 3:6-13 (NIV)

[6] *When the woman saw that the fruit of the tree was good for food and pleasing to the eye, and also desirable for gaining wisdom, she took some and ate it. She also gave some to her husband, who was with her, and he ate it.* [7] *Then the eyes of both of them were opened, and they realized they were naked; so they sewed fig leaves together and made coverings for themselves.*

[8] *Then the man and his wife heard the sound of the Lord God as he was walking in the garden in the cool of the day, and they hid from the Lord God among the trees of the garden.* [9] *But the Lord God called to the man, "Where are you?"*

[10] *He answered, "I heard you in the garden, and I was afraid because I was naked; so I hid."*

[11] *And he said, "Who told you that you were naked? Have you eaten from the tree that I commanded you not to eat from?"*

[12] *The man said, "The woman you put here with me—she gave me some fruit from the tree, and I ate it."*

[13] *Then the Lord God said to the woman, "What is this you have done?"*

The woman said, "The serpent deceived me, and I ate."

When Adam and Eve first sinned and "rebelled" against God, they at first tried to hide from Him, but of course you can't hide from God. Then they tried to blame each other or the serpent, but the truth was it was their fault. They needed to own what they did and take responsibility for it.

<u>Discussion Question:</u> Do you feel like you always take responsibility for what you do? Can you think of a time recently when you tried to blame someone else, but deep down you knew you had done wrong?

Baptism is about taking responsibility for what you have done wrong, but also admitting that your sin is something that you need help to overcome. There is a price to sin that is probably worse than we expected, and that's what God explained when He told Adam and Eve the consequence of their sin.

Genesis 3:16-19 (NIV)
[16] To the woman he said, "I will make your pains in childbearing very severe; with painful labor you will give birth to children. Your desire will be for your husband, and he will rule over you."
[17] To Adam he said, "Because you listened to your wife and ate fruit from the tree about which I commanded you, 'You must not eat from it,' "Cursed is the ground because of you; through painful toil you will eat food from it all the days of your life. [18] It will produce thorns and thistles for you, and you will eat the plants of the field. [19] By the sweat of your brow you will eat your food until you return to the ground, since from it you were taken; for dust you are and to dust you will return."

God told Adam in Genesis 2:17 that if he ate from the tree of the knowledge of good and evil, he would surely die. Yet after Adam and Eve sinned by eating from that tree, they didn't die right away. God told them they would eventually die – "to dust you shall return" – but before that happened, God explained how their relationship with each other and the earth would never be the same nor nearly as good as it was in Eden. And then God kicked them out of Eden because that is where the tree of life was, and because they sinned, they had chosen death and lost their access to eternal life.

<u>Discussion Question:</u> Why do you think Adam and Eve didn't immediately die when they sinned, even though God had said they would surely die?

- Adam and Eve didn't drop dead right away because God was not just talking about physical death, but spiritual death. Sin causes an invisible but mortal wound inside us spiritually that we might not see immediately, but it is real. A "mortal wound" is a wound that doesn't kill you right away, but it is so bad, that you will soon die. Once we have sinned, we have a mortal wound inside us spiritually, and death has a claim on us.

It turns out God told us the truth from the very beginning: If you sin, you will surely die.

Romans 5:12 (NIV1984) [12]*. . . sin entered the world through one man, and death through sin, and in this way death came to all men, because all sinned . . .*

Sin does more than bring death. Sin is slavery.

John 8:34 (NIV1984)
[34]*Jesus replied, "I tell you the truth, everyone who sins is a slave to sin.*

Discussion Question: Why do you think Jesus described sin like being a slave? Have you ever felt that way after doing something wrong?

- A common example is lying. When we tell a lie, we often have to tell that same lie again, or another lie, to try to avoid getting caught in our first lie. Pretty soon we are stuck or "enslaved" to keeping that lie going, and as we do, the consequences of that deception often get progressively worse.
- Another example is how if you cheat once and get away with it, it is much easier to decide to cheat again. After a while, you just naturally start cheating on all your tests or your homework as a habit, and it gets harder and harder to break that habit. You start depending on cheating.
- Yet another example is addiction. People who are addicted to drugs or alcohol would probably admit that it feels like slavery.

So, here is what we have learned about the nature of sin:

Sin is rebellion against God. It is like saying that we don't trust God, or we want something else more than we want to please or obey God. When we sin, something invisible and dreadful happens to us. We damage or break something spiritually, and we can't fix it on our own and we can't pay for the damage we caused, but unless the price is paid and the damage is fixed, death has a claim on us. We are enslaved by sin and death, and need God's help to break free.

#2 REPENTANCE

We turn from sin and turn toward God

We have already learned that sin is the problem that we must overcome. Sin is like turning away from God, and when we turn away from God - the giver of all life and all good things - we break things inside us spiritually that must be fixed.

Discussion Question: If turning away from God is what causes sin and everything that comes with it, then what would make sense as the solution to sin?

- To turn towards God again. That turning towards God is called *repentance.*

Do you want to get well?

To start our discussion of how we can be healed of sin, let's read the story of a time that Jesus healed a crippled man. Pay attention to the question that Jesus asks this crippled man.

John 5:1-6 (NIV)

Some time later, Jesus went up to Jerusalem for one of the Jewish festivals. [2] *Now there is in Jerusalem near the Sheep Gate a pool, which in Aramaic is called Bethesda and which is surrounded by five covered colonnades.* [3] *Here a great number of disabled people used to lie—the blind, the lame, the paralyzed.* [5] *One who was there had been an invalid for thirty-eight years.* [6] *When Jesus saw him lying there and learned that he had been in this condition for a long time, he asked him, "Do you want to get well?"*

<u>Discussion Question:</u> "Do you want to get well?" is a strange question to ask a crippled man. Why ask this? What does Jesus want this man to think about when answering?

- Being well would involve some trade-offs. He would have to accept some changes that could prove difficult, such as working again and being responsible for things he wasn't before.

Much like this crippled man, we have a serious problem: the "mortal wound" of sin. And just like this crippled man, the one who can heal us is Jesus. But we have to *want* to get well. We have to believe there is no other way except through Jesus. And we have to be willing to embrace the new responsibilities and life changes that will come with being healed by Christ.

<u>Discussion Question:</u> Repenting is like our way of saying we want to get well, we want to be healed from sin, but there is more to it than that. It is more than just saying we are sorry for our sins. The word *repent* means to turn or change. What do you think you would have to turn from? What changes do you think being a Christian will require of you?

Let's look at what Jesus told a few people they would have to change or give up.

Matthew 19:16-22 (NIV)

[16] *Just then a man came up to Jesus and asked, "Teacher, what good thing must I do to get eternal life?"*

[17] *"Why do you ask me about what is good?" Jesus replied. "There is only One who is good. If you want to enter life, keep the commandments."*

[18] *"Which ones?" he inquired.*

Jesus replied, "'You shall not murder, you shall not commit adultery, you shall not steal, you shall not give false testimony, [19] *honor your father and mother,' and 'love your neighbor as yourself.'"*

[20] *"All these I have kept," the young man said. "What do I still lack?"*

[21] *Jesus answered, "If you want to be perfect, go, sell your possessions and give to the poor, and you will have treasure in heaven. Then come, follow me."*

[22] *When the young man heard this, he went away sad, because he had great wealth.*

The point of this story is not that Jesus asks everyone who follows him to sell all they have and give it away. That is what Jesus asked of this young man because he loved possessions more than Jesus. For us, it may be something else that we would struggle to give up. The point is we should value Jesus and his truth and his forgiveness more than anything else. That is what Jesus taught some people who said they wanted to be his disciples:

Matthew 10:37-39 (NIV)

[37] *"Anyone who loves their father or mother more than me is not worthy of me; anyone who loves their son or daughter more than me is not worthy of me.* [38] *Whoever does not take up their cross and follow me is not worthy of me.* [39] *Whoever finds their life will lose it, and whoever loses their life for my sake will find it.*

<u>Discussion Question:</u> Is there anything you have that you would say is more important than following Jesus?

When we repent, we are not just turning from sin; we are turning the direction of our lives too, and submitting our plans to God's plans.

It is common in the Bible for people's plans and priorities to be drastically changed once they commit to following God.

<u>Discussion Question:</u> Can you think of some people in the Bible whose lives were drastically changed once they were called by God or obeyed God? How did their lives take unexpected turns?

- [The following examples are some of the many possible answers.]
- Even though Joseph did nothing wrong, he was sold by his jealous brothers into slavery. But he stayed faithful, and God finally rewarded him by making him the second most powerful man in Egypt.
- Moses was living a quiet life as a shepherd when God called him to travel to Egypt and lead the Israelites out of slavery. From that point on, Moses was involved in some of the most amazing events in human history, including the parting of the Red Sea and receiving the Ten Commandments from God.
- Esther was just a common Jewish girl living in a foreign land. Through circumstances no one could have predicted, she was chosen to be queen, and because of her position as queen, she was able to save her people from persecution.

Paul is another Bible character whose life changed drastically after he became a Christian. He went from persecuting Christians to being a Christian missionary, and eventually spent years in prison because of his faith. Here is what he says about everything he gave up and suffered after he gave his life to Christ:

Philippians 3:7-8 (NIV)
But whatever were gains to me I now consider loss for the sake of Christ. What is more, I consider everything a loss because of the surpassing worth of knowing Christ Jesus my Lord, for whose sake I have lost all things. I consider them garbage, that I may gain Christ . . .

All of these people could not have imagined how their lives would change and what would happen to them once they committed to obeying God. All of them had to make some sacrifices and give up some things for the sake of following God, but all of them would tell you now that it was completely worth it.

Turning from sin towards God will require some changes and sacrifices. You might already know of some changes you need to make, but other things will be asked of you that you probably can't anticipate yet.

It is hard to say how your life will change, or what turning towards Christ will cost you. You need to decide now, before you make that commitment, that you are willing to give up or invest whatever it may take. Jesus wants you to think about that and make sure you are ready to do that before you are baptized. But he also promises that if you do have to give up some friends, or change your life plans, or sacrifice what you want to do at times, he promises that whatever following him costs, it is worth it:

Matthew 19:29 (NLT) [29] *And everyone who has given up houses or brothers or sisters or father or mother or children or property, for my sake, will receive a hundred times as much in return and will inherit eternal life.*

Discussion Question: What are your plans and dreams right now for what you want to do with the rest of your life? Talk about your goals, and where you want to live, and what you want to accomplish. What are some ways you can see God using you in those plans?

So, here is what we have learned about repentance:

Repentance is turning from sin and turning towards God. We turn towards God because we have sinned against Him and He is the only one who can forgive us and fix our problem of sin. Repentance is also turning towards a new mission or purpose in life. When we repent, we are saying that we understand this will require some changes and sacrifices from us, and we don't know how God may use us or change our lives, but we are willing to let Him use us because nothing is more valuable to us than living with Him and for Him.

#3 SAVED BY CHRIST

God sent Jesus as the answer to our sin problem

We have learned that when we sin, even when we think it is not a big deal, it is actually rebellion against God, and that is serious. Our sin means we have a "mortal wound" spiritually, and unless that is healed, we will be forever separated from God when we die.

Healing our sin problem requires more than just trying to do better. We still have that wound inside, and we still have broken something spiritually that we cannot fix. Think of it like when you drip ice cream on your shirt. Even if you never eat ice cream again, you still have a stain on your shirt. You must do something proactive to get that shirt clean again.

We have to go to God to erase the stain of sin in our lives. The good news is that He wants to help us. To make that happen, he sent Jesus.

John 3:16 (NIV1984)

[16] "For God so loved the world that he gave his one and only Son, that whoever believes in him shall not perish but have eternal life.

Romans 6:23 (HCSB)

For the wages of sin is death, but the gift of God is eternal life in Christ Jesus our Lord.

Jesus came to forgive our sins, which would fix what was broken, and to pay the debt we owed to death so that it could no longer be held against us.

Forgiveness requires sacrifice

To understand how Jesus did that, you need to know about the link between sin and death, and forgiveness and sacrifice. We have already seen that there is always a price for sin. Sin causes damages, and the worst of all those damages is death. "The wages of sin is death." To forgive those sins and pay the damages or debt caused by sin also has a price.

Discussion Question: Think about when someone has forgiven you of something that you owed, or something that you did wrong. When they forgave you, what did it cost them? Did they have to give up something?

- If you owe your friend $20, but he tells you not to worry about it, then he has forgiven you a debt, but that also means he won't ever see that money you owe him. When a debt is forgiven, that means someone will not collect the money due them. It costs them the value of the loan.
- If someone forgives you when you have done wrong, it may mean that they have to pay a price you could not. Many times parents must pay to fix a broken window or a wrecked car or something similar that their children broke, but that their children cannot pay to fix themselves.

From the very beginning, sin has always caused damage, and that damage had a price, and so to forgive that sin also has a price. The price of forgiveness in the Bible is often represented as a sacrifice. The first example of this is seen right after Adam and Eve committed the first sin in Eden.

Genesis 3:7 (NLT)

[7] At that moment their eyes were opened, and they suddenly felt shame at their nakedness. So they sewed fig leaves together to cover themselves.

They were ashamed and tried to cover their shame with leaves. God took pity on them and gave them better clothing made of animal skins (Genesis 3:21). But think about what that meant: animals had to die to provide the skins that covered their shame.

That was the first preview of the system of animal sacrifices that God would dictate through Moses. In the Mosaic Law, the people offered various animals as sacrifices for their sins. The death of that animal was a reminder that sin has a price, and so does forgiveness. An animal was sacrificed to cover the shame and cost of sin.

Under the Mosaic Law, once a year, on the Day of Atonement, the High Priest would bring two goats before God. One was killed as a sacrifice. The priest laid his hands on the other goat to signify that all the sins of the people were symbolically placed on it, and then that goat was set free into the wilderness. It carried the sins of the people away from them.

Two things happened on the Day of Atonement: a sacrifice was made – something died as the price of sin – and sin was carried away. Remember that. That is important, because all those sacrifices were a preview of what Jesus would do for our sins.

Hebrews 10:1-7 (NLT)

The old system under the law of Moses was only a shadow, a dim preview of the good things to come, not the good things themselves. The sacrifices under that system were repeated again and again, year after year, but they were never able to provide perfect cleansing for those who came to worship. 2 If they could have provided perfect cleansing, the sacrifices would have stopped, for the worshipers would have been purified once for all time, and their feelings of guilt would have disappeared.

3 But instead, those sacrifices actually reminded them of their sins year after year. 4 For it is not possible for the blood of bulls and goats to take away sins. 5 That is why, when Christ came into the world, he said to God,

"You did not want animal sacrifices or sin offerings.
But you have given me a body to offer.
6 You were not pleased with burnt offerings or other offerings for sin.
7 Then I said, 'Look, I have come to do your will, O God—
as is written about me in the Scriptures.'"

The animal sacrifices were a reminder of the price of sin and forgiveness, but an animal is not an adequate substitution for a human. To pay our debt caused by our sin, Jesus himself agreed to die –that is how the debt to death had to be paid once and for all. He had to come in human form so he could die for us.

Hebrews 2:14-15 (NLT)

14 Because God's children are human beings—made of flesh and blood—the Son also became flesh and blood. For only as a human being could he die, and only by dying could he break the power of the devil, who had the power of death. 15 Only in this way could he set free all who have lived their lives as slaves to the fear of dying.

Jesus didn't die because he committed any sin. He died to pay the price for our sin. He became the sacrifice, like on the Day of Atonement, and he carried our sins far away from us, just like that goat in the Old Testament that carried the people's sins into the wilderness, never to be seen again.

Now here is something important that you need to understand about this: When Jesus died as a sacrifice for our sins, he did not die because he sinned. He also did not become sinful by taking on our sins.

1 John 3:5 (NLT)
[5] And you know that Jesus came to take away our sins, and there is no sin in him.

Some people are confused about what happened on the cross with Christ because of this verse:

2 Corinthians 5:21 (ESV)
[21] For our sake he made him to be sin who knew no sin, so that in him we might become the righteousness of God.

How could Jesus become sin but remain the holy God? If all of our sins were placed on him on the cross, how could he remain holy? He couldn't. So what do we do with 2 Corinthians 5:21? A couple other verses better clarify what "he made him to be sin" means.

1 Peter 2:24 (ESV)
[24] He himself bore our sins in his body on the tree, that we might die to sin and live to righteousness. By his wounds you have been healed.

The Greek word translated as *bore* is anapherō, which means to take or carry up. Just like the scapegoat symbolically carried the sins away on the Day of Atonement, Christ carried our sins to the cross.

You see the same idea in **Isaiah 53:4-5 (ESV):**
[4] Surely he has borne our griefs and carried our sorrows; yet we esteemed him stricken, smitten by God, and afflicted. But he was wounded for our transgressions; he was crushed for our iniquities; upon him was the chastisement that brought us peace, and with his stripes we are healed.

Jesus was and is and always will be the perfectly holy and sinless Son of God. But he was carrying, he was bearing, our sins on the cross. While carrying those sins, he took the consequence for them – which was death - that rightfully belong to sinners. That's why 2 Corinthians says "he made Jesus to be sin who knew no sin." That doesn't mean he was sinful, but that in carrying those sins, he was representative of sin and its consequences.

So Jesus carried our sins up to the cross, and he was nailed to the cross, carrying our sins. Do you know what happened to our sins? They were nailed to the cross too.

Colossians 2:13-14 (NLT)
[13] You were dead because of your sins and because your sinful nature was not yet cut away. Then God made you alive with Christ, for he forgave all our sins. [14] He canceled the record of the charges against us and took it away by nailing it to the cross.

Jesus carried our sins up on the cross, and when they nailed him to the cross, they were nailing those sins, those charges, those shameful deeds too. They were left on that cross, cancelled, paid. A paid bill has no power, it is nothing to fear. Satan can no longer use our sins to accuse us.

By dying as he did for us, Jesus volunteered to be the sacrifice that would once and for all forgive us of our sins.

Hebrews 10:14 (NIV)
[14] For by one sacrifice he has made perfect forever those who are being made holy.

Jesus' sacrifice created this safe place where the price we could not pay was paid. Baptism is how we enter that safe place. We can think of baptism as the one safe place in all of the earth where we can get rid of our sins and break the claim that death has on us because of our sins. If we go to that safe place of baptism, Satan and death have no claim on us. In baptism, we bring our sins and leave them there, where they are paid for.

Baptism is how we accept the forgiveness that Jesus offers us.

Jesus voluntarily died for us as a sacrifice to forgive our sins, heal that mortal wound in our souls, and therefore free us from death. That is what Jesus did to save us from sin. Baptism is what we do to accept the forgiveness that Jesus offers. The neat thing is that baptism physically reminds us of what Jesus did, and by "acting it out," we are joining ourselves to Christ.

Jesus died on the cross to forgive us and cancel the grip sin had on us. His body was buried in a grave for three days. When we go under the water, that mimics how Jesus went down into the grave. The water of baptism is like a grave, where we bury all our sins and our old selves.

After three days, Jesus rose from his grave. He overcame death because death had no hold on him. In the same way, we come up out of the water as a new person in many ways, and death no longer has a hold on us either. We no longer have that spiritual wound because of our sin. We will one day go to live with God forever, just like Jesus did.

Here is how Paul summed up everything that happens in baptism:

Romans 6:3-11 (NLT)
[3] Or have you forgotten that when we were joined with Christ Jesus in baptism, we joined him in his death? [4] For we died and were buried with Christ by baptism. And just as Christ was raised from the dead by the glorious power of the Father, now we also may live new lives.

[5] Since we have been united with him in his death, we will also be raised to life as he was. [6] We know that our old sinful selves were crucified with Christ so that sin might lose its power in our lives. We are no longer slaves to sin. [7] For when we died with Christ we were set free from the power of sin.[8] And since we died with Christ, we know we will also live with him.

[9] We are sure of this because Christ was raised from the dead, and he will never die again. Death no longer has any power over him.[10] When he died, he died once to break the power of sin. But now that he lives, he lives for the glory of God. [11] So you also should consider yourselves to be dead to the power of sin and alive to God through Christ Jesus.

So what we were – the "old man of sin" is what some people call it – is now dead and buried at the bottom of the water. We buried what we don't want to be anymore, and we come up out of the water to live a new life in Christ.

Colossians 3:3-4 (ESV)
[3] For you have died, and your life is hidden with Christ in God.[4] When Christ who is your life appears, then you also will appear with him in glory.

If it helps, picture yourself hidden in Christ, picture yourself inside his strong arms, and in him, the devil and death have no claim.

Discussion Question: Where have you felt the most safe and secure? What gives you a sense of protection and strength?

Well, once you have been baptized, God promises you are in the safest place you can be spiritually. Death has no claim on you. Your sins have been buried and Satan can't use them against you and now there is nothing separating you from God. The big change that you must understand is that you are forgiven and free, and now you don't owe Satan or sin anything. You no longer are a slave to sin like before.

Romans 8:1-2 (ESV) *There is therefore now no condemnation for those who are in Christ Jesus. [2] For the law of the Spirit of life has set you free in Christ Jesus from the law of sin and death.*

So, here is what we have learned about salvation:

God told us that it was necessary for Christ to come and die to pay our debt and fix what we broke spiritually by our sin. Jesus' sacrifice on the cross created a place where the debt to death was paid, so the Devil and death had no claim. We can think of baptism as the one safe place in all of the earth where we can get rid of our sins. Baptism mimics how we are joining ourselves to Jesus. We take our sins down under the water like Jesus was laid in the grave; we come out of the water forgiven and free to live with God, just like Jesus rose from the grave and returned to live forever with God.

[Below is some supplementary material that addresses a couple of questions or misconceptions about what happened on the cross. If these are not questions for the person you are studying with, skip this and go on to lesson #4 "BY BELIEVING".]

If Jesus is part of the trinity, how did God forsake him on the cross?

This comes from **Matthew 27:46 (ESV)**

[46] And about the ninth hour Jesus cried out with a loud voice, saying, "Eli, Eli, lema sabachthani?" that is, "My God, my God, why have you forsaken me?"

If Jesus is part of the trinity, how can one part of God turn its back on another part? How can God separate like that?

He didn't. God never forsook Jesus, or turned away from him, or shut him off in any way.

You may have been taught that God turned His back on Jesus because Jesus became sin, and God cannot tolerate sin, so all God's wrath came down on Jesus and He forsook him. But as we have already learned, Jesus did not become sinful. So God the Father turning his back or tearing away from Jesus is not necessary or consistent with what scripture says about the nature of the trinity.

"My God, My God, why have you forsaken me?" is a quote from the first line of Psalm 22. Jesus is quoting scripture, and he's doing that so that his disciples and the Jewish leaders present would put what they were seeing at Calvary in context of that Psalm. Jesus is telling them that what they are witnessing was prophesied by David.

Listen to some of the verses from that psalm:

"All who see me mock me . . . He trusts in the Lord; let him deliver him; let him rescue him!"

"They have pierced my hands and feet"

"They divide my garments among them, and for my clothing they cast lots."

All of those things were happening as they watched. And that psalm ends as a song of victory; it is a song of trust in God. God did not forsake Jesus. In fact one line of Psalm 22 says, *"For he [God] has not despised or abhorred the affliction of the afflicted, and he has not hidden his face from him, but has heard, when he cried to him."*

That is consistent with what Jesus confidently told his disciples just hours before his arrest:

John 16:32 (NIV)
32 "A time is coming and in fact has come when you will be scattered, each to your own home. You will leave me all alone. Yet I am not alone, for my Father is with me.

So God did not forsake Jesus. And that helps answer the next question:

Did Jesus go to Hell after he died?

The reasoning behind this is that if Jesus became all of our sins, when he died, he took our sins with him there. He paid the price we otherwise would have paid to Hell.

This was a doctrine seen in what was called The Apostles' Creed, which said Jesus:

> . . .suffered under Pontius Pilate, was crucified, died, and was buried. He descended into hell. On the third day he rose again from the dead. He ascended into heaven and is seated at the right hand of God the Father Almighty.

The problem is there is nothing in scripture that directly says this. This creed came in full form 700 years after Jesus' death and was based on the sequence of events that some people assumed about Jesus' death, plus a couple of difficult scriptures in 1st Peter that must be carefully interpreted in context.

Even though that statement was dropped in the Nicene Creed, this belief was seen in iconography and reinforced by Dante's *Inferno*, which has been very influential in painting our conception of Hell. Dante described how everything in Hell is cracked and broken, like it had been hit by an earthquake. The stairs are broken, the pillars are leaning. Dante used that in his description because of what is described as the "harrowing of Hell," which is the belief that Jesus died, and carried all sin to the pit of Hell. When he rose on the third day and conquered death, he ripped through Hell and shook its very foundations as an eternal reminder that this place has lost, that it has been overcome by Jesus.

That has popular appeal among some fellowships, but it's not scriptural. We've already shown that Jesus was never sinful, so Jesus was not required to go to Hell. He has no obligations to Hell. Satan has never had any power over the Son of God.

Besides that, we do have some scriptures that are quite clear what happens to Jesus after he dies on the cross.

Luke 23:42-43, 46 (ESV)

42 And he said, "Jesus, remember me when you come into your kingdom." 43 And he said to him, "Truly, I say to you, today you will be with me in Paradise."

46 Then Jesus, calling out with a loud voice, said, "Father, into your hands I commit my spirit!" And having said this he breathed his last.

Jesus tells the criminal on the cross next to him that today he would be with him in Paradise. And the last words of Jesus make clear that Jesus' spirit was in the Heavenly Father's hands.

When Jesus tells Mary Magdalene at the empty tomb does not contradict that:

John 20:17 (NIV)

[17] Jesus said, "Do not hold on to me, for I have not yet ascended to the Father. Go instead to my brothers and tell them, 'I am ascending to my Father and your Father, to my God and your God.'"

He is simply saying he has not ascended in bodily form. She does not need to cling to him because he will be around for another forty days, and only then will he ascend to the heavens.

What we can say about these questions, based on scripture, is that it's obvious Jesus is in complete control to the very end, and he voluntarily decided when he was going to die (John 10:17-18), and when his human body died, he was going to Heaven, not Hell.

#4 BY BELIEVING
How do we know this works?

So when you are baptized and come out of the water, how do you know this all worked? What proof do you have that you are forgiven?

Many people say that they feel like a weight has been lifted off them, or they have an unmistakable sense of being clean. But other people are baptized and don't feel anything. That is okay too. It doesn't mean their baptism didn't count. We aren't promised in the Bible that we will feel a particular feeling when we come out of the water.

Many times, it is impossible at first to tell that anything has changed. The person in the water is now just wet. So if we can't count on a certain feeling, if there is no flash of light or voice from Heaven, then how do we know this really worked? How do we know that after we are baptized, we are really forgiven and the claim of death on us has been broken?

Romans 6:8-9 (NLT)
[8] And since we died with Christ, we know we will also live with him.[9] We are sure of this because Christ was raised from the dead, and he will never die again. Death no longer has any power over him

Discussion Question: What does this verse tell us is the proof that baptism frees us from the debt we had to death?

- The proof this works is in Christ's resurrection. Many times the New Testament says that the resurrection of Jesus is so important because that miracle was meant to prove that God will do the same for us as He did for Jesus – He will empower us to rise again after we die.

1 Corinthians 15:14, 20-26 (NIV) *[14] And if Christ has not been raised, our preaching is useless and so is your faith . . . [20] But Christ has indeed been raised from the dead, the firstfruits of those who have fallen asleep. [21] For since death came through a man, the resurrection of the dead comes also through a man. [22] For as in Adam all die, so in Christ all will be made alive . . .*

[23] But each in his own turn: Christ, the firstfruits; then, when he comes, those who belong to him.[24] Then the end will come, when he hands over the kingdom to God the Father after he has destroyed all dominion, authority and power.[25] For he must reign until he has put all his enemies under his feet.[26] The last enemy to be destroyed is death.

These and several other verses view the resurrection of Christ as the preview of what will happen to us once we have been forgiven. Once we are baptized, we will still one day die physically. That's part of living in this broken world. But we don't have to fear it, and after that, death has nothing with which to hold us. After we die, we will live again with God, and we will live forever, just like Jesus did when he conquered death and rose again three days later. He is now ruling in Heaven, and that is where we will be, united with him forever.

This only works, though, if you believe.

Christ points to his resurrection as proof that you can trust him when he says he can forgive your sins, and that death no longer has a claim on you. Christ has done what only he could do to forgive our sins. But we still have a part to play, too. Because of Christ, baptism works, but it only works if you believe.

John 20:30-31 (ESV)
[30] Now Jesus did many other signs in the presence of the disciples, which are not written in this book;[31] but these are written so that you may believe that Jesus is the Christ, the Son of God, and that by believing you may have life in his name.

John 3:16-18 (NIV)
[16] "For God so loved the world that he gave his one and only Son, that whoever believes in him shall not perish but have eternal life. [17] For God did not send his Son into the world to condemn the world, but to save the world through him. [18] Whoever believes in him is not condemned, but whoever does not believe stands condemned already because he has not believed in the name of God's one and only Son.

<u>Discussion Question:</u> What do you think is the difference between *knowing about* Jesus and *believing* in Jesus?

- Many people know about Jesus, but don't believe in him. Even many other religions believe Jesus existed and was a "good teacher," but they don't believe *in* him.
- Belief means that we accept his teaching as truth, which excludes anything contrary to Jesus' teachings. When you believe, you are choosing sides. You are saying that you will not mix what Jesus taught with other religions or belief systems because Jesus speaks for God.
- The other big difference between belief and knowing is that belief involves us. Belief requires change or action. A familiar illustration of this is a rope. You can say you believe the rope is strong, but true belief is when you are willing to hang from that rope over the edge of a cliff.

Before you get baptized, someone may ask you to make a "confession," and often it is as simple as this: they will ask you if you believe Jesus is the Christ, the son of God. That may sound like a strange question, but that question is meant to encompass all that is true about Jesus.

When we are baptized, we are declaring that we believe Jesus, and believe in Jesus. We believe he really is the Son of God who speaks with the authority of God. We believe he really did all the miracles recorded in the gospels. We believe he really can forgive our sins, and that he died for us and rose from the dead to prove his power to forgive us. What we show by making that "confession" and being baptized is that we don't just know about Jesus, but that we really believe and trust in Jesus.

<u>Discussion Question:</u> Believing in Jesus doesn't mean you will know everything about Jesus right now, but based on what you do know about Jesus from the Bible, what are the things that you don't understand about him or what he did? Is there anything that the New Testament says about Jesus that you just don't find believable?

- Remember, there is a difference between not understanding and not believing. You may not understand something Jesus did or said, but still believe he said it or still believe that it is true.

God gives the gift of forgiveness and grace to those who believe and obey. There is no magic in the water when you are baptized. The power to forgive our sins and free us from death is in God alone, and He gives it to us in that water because we believe.

Colossians 2:12 (ESV)

[12] having been buried with him in baptism, in which you were also raised with him through faith in the powerful working of God, who raised him from the dead.

There are things about the salvation process that we probably can't fully explain or understand, but that is alright so long as we have faith that God has the power to do what He promises. What God looks for in us is faith and obedience.

Discussion Question: There are many things in life that we see or use every day, and we can't fully explain how they work, but we still believe in or trust in them. Can you think of any examples?

- When you get on an airplane, you are trusting your life to the belief that plane can fly, even though you probably can't explain exactly how it works.
- There are all sorts of examples of technology that we depend on but can't explain. How exactly does a cell phone, or wireless internet, or the radio waves that produce sound in our car stereo work? How exactly does the medicine you take work? Even though you expect them to work, can you really explain exactly how they work?

This works because God says it will.

We believe many things that we can't explain because we trust what people tell us about them. We trust that if a doctor says a medicine will make us better, it will, not because we understand how the medicine works, but because we trust that doctor and what he knows about medicine.

In the same way, when we are baptized for the forgiveness of our sins, we do so not because we can fully explain how it works, but because we trust God who tells us it will.

There is a story in the Old Testament, in Exodus 12, that is a kind of preview of what God does for us in baptism, but that also illustrates the role of belief in things we can't explain.

In that story, God's people, the Israelites, were still enslaved in Egypt, but God had been using various plagues to pressure the Egyptians to free the Israelites. Because pharaoh kept refusing, God finally resorted to one last, terrible plague: every firstborn male in Egypt – human and livestock – would die on the same night. God would send an angel to kill them. The penalty of death was coming because of Pharaoh's refusal to obey God.

But God told the Israelites that this plague would not touch them if they did something rather strange. Every family was to kill a lamb and cook it so they would have food for the journey they were about to take out of Egypt. But the strange part was they were to smear the blood of that lamb on the doorframes of their homes. When the angel of death came to any house covered by that blood, it would pass over, which is how the Hebrew tradition of Passover began.

Exodus 12:12-13 (NIV)

[12] "On that same night I will pass through Egypt and strike down every firstborn of both people and animals, and I will bring judgment on all the gods of Egypt. I am the Lord. [13] The blood will be a sign for you on the houses where you are, and when I see the blood, I will pass over you. No destructive plague will touch you when I strike Egypt.

Now there are some direct parallels between that story and baptism. Jesus is called the lamb of God, sacrificed for us, and he died on Passover. It is his blood that "covers" us from sin. But notice too that the blood on the doorframe only worked that way because God said it would. We don't know why that worked except that the people believed what God told them, and they lived.

The first sin happened because Adam and Eve did not believe what God told them. That introduced death into the world. We'll only be forgiven and live if we do believe what God tells us. And what He tells us is that to be forgiven and freed from the debt of death, we need to be baptized. We just need to be obedient and believe that.

So here is what we learned about the role of belief in baptism:

To accept the forgiveness and hope offered by Christ, we must believe in him. That is why we are often asked to make a "confession" of our belief that Jesus is the Son of God. We are expressing not just that we believe Jesus existed, but that he truly is our only hope for forgiveness. We believe in him as our truth, and we will follow him only, not mixing him with other religions or belief systems. There are things about salvation that we may not understand, but we trust in God's plan for us, which includes baptism.

#4 WHAT NEXT?
you are given help to be holy

So what is different after you are baptized? Like we said earlier, not everyone feels differently right after they are baptized. We aren't promised we will feel a certain way. But whether we sense it or not, some important things happen in baptism, and you are not the same person afterward. We'll look at some scriptures about what changes after you are baptized.

You are freed from sin

When Peter tells the crowd at Pentecost to repent and be baptized, he promises that two things will happen for them:

Acts 2:38 (NIV)
[38] Peter replied, "Repent and be baptized, every one of you, in the name of Jesus Christ for the forgiveness of your sins. And you will receive the gift of the Holy Spirit.

The first thing he promises is that their sins will be forgiven. That means that all the sins you have committed up until you are baptized are erased, wiped clean, and will not be held against you by God.

Hebrews assures us that the sacrifice of Christ is powerful enough to forgive our sins – all sins – once and for all.

Hebrews 10:10 (HCSB)
[10] By this will of God, we have been sanctified through the offering of the body of Jesus Christ once and for all.

But even better, that forgiveness is applied forward in time, too, so that whenever you sin after you are baptized, you are forgiven of those too. Christ's forgiveness works backwards and forwards.

Hebrews 7:25 (NIV)
[25] Therefore he is able to save completely those who come to God through him, because he always lives to intercede for them.

1 John 2:1-2 (NIV)
My dear children, I write this to you so that you will not sin. But if anybody does sin, we have an advocate with the Father—Jesus Christ, the Righteous One. [2] He is the atoning sacrifice for our sins, and not only for ours but also for the sins of the whole world.

So will you still sin after you are baptized? Will you still make bad choices sometimes? Yes. The verse above is honest about that. But listen, here is the big difference after you are baptized: your relationship to sin has changed. Remember how Jesus described sin as slavery? Well, when you are baptized, you are no longer a slave to sin.

Romans 6:17-18 (NIV)
[17] But thanks be to God that, though you used to be slaves to sin, you have come to obey from your heart the pattern of teaching that has now claimed your allegiance. [18] You have been set free from sin and have become slaves to righteousness.

Our very *nature* is changed because Christ has cut us free from our old, unspiritual, sinful nature. Paul talks a lot about this change in the letter of Colossians. He says that when we are baptized, our nature – how we are inside – is changed.

Colossians 2:10-12 (NIV)
In him you were also circumcised with a circumcision not performed by human hands. Your whole self ruled by the flesh was put off when you were circumcised by Christ, having been buried with him in baptism, in which you were also raised with him through your faith in the working of God, who raised him from the dead.

Because of that change in our nature, we now can say no to sin because we don't owe sin anything. We are not doomed to be overcome by the same old temptations; it is no longer a given that we will give in to sin!

Colossians 3:1-10 (NIV)

Since, then, you have been raised with Christ, set your hearts on things above, where Christ is, seated at the right hand of God. [2] *Set your minds on things above, not on earthly things.* [3] *For you died, and your life is now hidden with Christ in God.* [4] *When Christ, who is your life, appears, then you also will appear with him in glory.*

[5] *Put to death, therefore, whatever belongs to your earthly nature: sexual immorality, impurity, lust, evil desires and greed, which is idolatry.*

[6] *Because of these, the wrath of God is coming.* [7] *You used to walk in these ways, in the life you once lived.* [8] *But now you must also rid yourselves of all such things as these: anger, rage, malice, slander, and filthy language from your lips.* [9] *Do not lie to each other, since you have taken off your old self with its practices* [10] *and have put on the new self, which is being renewed in knowledge in the image of its Creator.*

Christ has overcome. Christ has knocked down every hurdle so we can grow up into our "new self" who is holy. The only reason that we will not grow is if we refuse to, if we hang on to things that we don't have to.

The way that your identity is changed and your relationship to sin is changed is demonstrated in the familiar story of the prodigal son.

Luke 15:11-24 (NIV1984)

[11] *Jesus continued: "There was a man who had two sons.* [12] *The younger one said to his father, 'Father, give me my share of the estate.' So he divided his property between them.*

[13] *"Not long after that, the younger son got together all he had, set off for a distant country and there squandered his wealth in wild living.* [14] *After he had spent everything, there was a severe famine in that whole country, and he began to be in need.* [15] *So he went and hired himself out to a citizen of that country, who sent him to his fields to feed pigs.* [16] *He longed to fill his stomach with the pods that the pigs were eating, but no one gave him anything.*

[17] *"When he came to his senses, he said, 'How many of my father's hired men have food to spare, and here I am starving to death!* [18] *I will set out and go back to my father and say to him: Father, I have sinned against heaven and against you.* [19] *I am no longer worthy to be called your son; make me like one of your hired men.'* [20] *So he got up and went to his father.*

"But while he was still a long way off, his father saw him and was filled with compassion for him; he ran to his son, threw his arms around him and kissed him.

[21] *"The son said to him, 'Father, I have sinned against heaven and against you. I am no longer worthy to be called your son.'*

[22] *"But the father said to his servants, 'Quick! Bring the best robe and put it on him. Put a ring on his finger and sandals on his feet.* [23] *Bring the fattened calf and kill it. Let's have a feast and celebrate.* [24] *For this son of mine was dead and is alive again; he was lost and is found.' So they began to celebrate.*

<u>Discussion Question:</u> **Could you imagine the Prodigal Son, after he came home, deciding to run away again back to the pig sty? Can you imagine any reason he would do that?**

The son would be crazy to go back to starving on a pig farm when his father has forgiven him, welcomed him home, and given him such love. The pig sty is how we should view sin after we are baptized. We belong to the Father, and He has given us everything, and there is no reason we have to go back to the pigs ever. One of the reasons baptism is described as a death is to emphasize how we should view sin from that point on – we died to it, and know it has nothing to offer us. There is no good or even sane reason for returning to a life of sin.

When Christians do give in to sin, it is usually because they believed a lie. Satan is an excellent liar, and he will try to get you to believe lies about your Father God, or you, or the pig sty of sin.

Some lies about God may be something like "God won't care because this isn't that bad," or "God wants me to be happy more than anything."

The lies Satan will want you to believe about yourself could be: "I can't help it, this is how God made me," or "I deserve to have what I want."

And probably most often, he will want you to believe lies about sin itself:
"I'll just do it one more time."
"This doesn't hurt anyone."
"This must be ok because everyone is doing it."
"This time will be different."
"This isn't really so bad."

The more we live with the Father and learn from him, however, the better we get at seeing the truth and recognizing those lies and resisting them. But even better, we have a Helper from God living in us to do just that.

<u>Discussion Question:</u> **What do you think would be the most helpful thing to you as a new Christian? If there was a certain power you could have, or if you could know something that you don't now, what would it be?**

Christ doesn't just change our nature and our relationship to sin. He also sends a Helper to guide and encourage us in our new lives as disciples. Let's look again at what Peter promised to those who are baptized, because there was more there than just forgiveness.

Acts 2:38 (NIV)
[38] Peter replied, "Repent and be baptized, every one of you, in the name of Jesus Christ for the forgiveness of your sins. And you will receive the gift of the Holy Spirit.

We have a Helper

A full discussion of the Holy Spirit is beyond the scope of this book. For now, you just need to know that the Holy Spirit is a part of God. God is described as the "trinity," meaning three. God is a relationship. There is God the Father, God the Son, and God the Holy Spirit. That is very hard for us to grasp, but that is how God is revealed to us through scripture.

Jesus promised his disciples that he would send a Helper for them after he ascended back to Heaven. That Helper was the Holy Spirit. The Spirit came in very visible, supernatural ways in the first years of the church, empowering the apostles and those that the apostles laid hands on to do miraculous things, and heal, and speak in tongues. Those displays of power were another way of proving the truth of what they preached.

The Holy Spirit is promised to every Christian, as a helper and guide that abides in us. We may not experience the miraculous displays of the First Century, but here are some of the roles that scripture says the Spirit plays in our lives: he comforts (Acts 9:31); he teaches and reminds (1 Corinthians 12:3); he decides and directs (John 16:13 and Acts 8:29); he searches the thoughts of God (1 Corinthians 2:10-11) and helps us understand them; gives spiritual gifts (1 Corinthians 12:11); helps us in our prayers (Romans 8:26); and abides in us (John 14:17).

We've already learned from Colossians that our very nature is changed by Christ. Our old slavery to sin in "the flesh" has been cut away from us. We don't live like that anymore. Now we live in the Spirit.

Romans 8:8-9 (HCSB)
[8] Those who are in the flesh cannot please God. [9] You, however, are not in the flesh, but in the Spirit, since the Spirit of God lives in you.

That changes all the math in our struggle with sin. We're not just forgiven. We have something more. Jesus sends the Spirit to dwell in us to make a difference and apply that forgiveness in our lives. We are not just left on our own to try to do the best we can.

John 14:15-16 (ESV)

[16] And I will ask the Father, and he will give you another Helper, to be with you forever, [17] even the Spirit of truth, whom the world cannot receive, because it neither sees him nor knows him. You know him, for he dwells with you and will be in you.

Jesus calls the Spirit "The Helper" because he helps us do things we could not do on our own. He lives in believers and gives us a new advantage, a new opportunity, new capabilities that people outside of Christ just don't have.

That's because the defining characteristic of the Spirit is *power.* Jesus tells his disciples the Spirit will come in power. The Spirit empowers us do what we cannot do on our own. The Spirit gives us power that goes beyond what we can do in these bodies with their weaknesses.

Romans 8:12-16 (HCSB)

[12] So then, brothers, we are not obligated to the flesh to live according to the flesh, [13] for if you live according to the flesh, you are going to die. But if by the Spirit you put to death the deeds of the body, you will live. [14] All those led by God's Spirit are God's sons. [15] For you did not receive a spirit of slavery to fall back into fear, but you received the Spirit of adoption, by whom we cry out, "Abba, Father!" [16] The Spirit Himself testifies together with our spirit that we are God's children,

We have been changed. We have something we didn't before. In the Spirit, we have the power to put to death the sinful deeds of the body. This doesn't just mean we are forgiven. This is talking about actively cutting out and resisting sin as we go about living each day. Helped by the power of the Spirit, we are free to not sin. We have no obligation to sin. We are not enslaved to sin. Whatever those sins are that have had a tight grip on you, you can kill them, end them, through the Spirit.

You may not struggle with many sins right now. Truthfully, some sins won't ever be temptations to you, and some won't be temptations until later in your life. It is likely, though, that there are some temptations you will work on your whole life as a disciple, but overcoming sin and reflecting God's holiness is really possible through the Spirit.

There's one more thing about the Holy Spirit you need to know before we move on. It is in this verse:

1 John 4:13 (NLT)
[13] And God has given us his Spirit as proof that we live in him and he in us.

It's a sad thing for a Christian to go through life wondering, questioning, what will happen when he dies, hoping he is doing enough to be okay with God. The Spirit inside you should erase those doubts. When you are a baptized believer relying on the Spirit, you can be confident that you are one of God's children.

Romans 8:15-17 (NLT)
So you have not received a spirit that makes you fearful slaves. Instead, you received God's Spirit when he adopted you as his own children. Now we call him, "Abba, Father." For his Spirit joins with our spirit to affirm that we are God's children. And since we are his children, we are his heirs. In fact, together with Christ we are heirs of God's glory.

With the Spirit in you, if someone asks if you are going to Heaven when you die, your answer should not be "I think so . . . I hope so." The correct answer is a definite, resounding YES!

So here is what is different after baptism:

In Acts 2:38, Peter promises two things when we are baptized: forgiveness and the gift of the Holy Spirit. Christ's forgiveness works backwards and forwards, so that whenever you sin after you are baptized, you are forgiven of those sins too. One of the reasons baptism is described as a death is to emphasize how we should view sin from that point on – we died to it, and know it has nothing to offer us. Christ also sends a Helper to guide and encourage us in our new lives as disciples. Jesus sends the Spirit to dwell in us to make a difference and apply that forgiveness in our lives. We are not just left on our own to try to do the best we can.

#5 THE CHURCH
You are where you are for a reason

We've already learned about so many things that Christ has done for us to allow us to be forgiven and holy. In baptism, our nature is changed, and we are no longer slaves to sin. It is no longer a given that we will give in. Our very relationship to sin has changed.

To help us further, Christ sent the Holy Spirit as a helper to abide in us as a guide and counselor and comforter. God makes His power available to us through the Spirit to overcome sin and truly be holy.

But there is something else that Christ left behind to help us: the Church. You may already belong to a church, but after you are baptized, your role in church is a little different. It takes on a new level of accountability and responsibility.

The church is a wonderful, complex thing, so to explain our part in it and how it is meant to help us, the Bible compares the church to several different things that are already familiar to us, such as a body or a family. When we put all these word pictures and metaphors together, then we start to get a complete understanding of how important the church will be to us for the rest of our lives.

Welcome to the team

The first way we will describe your new place in the church is to compare it to being a new player on a team.

Galatians 3:26-29 (NLT)

For you are all children of God through faith in Christ Jesus. And all who have been united with Christ in baptism have put on Christ, like putting on new clothes. There is no longer Jew or Gentile, slave or free, male or female. For you are all one in Christ Jesus.

In baptism, we have all put on Christ like the players on a team all wear the same uniform. We are the same in that we have all "put on" Christ. Now you want what is best for everyone in the church. You are united with them, and in the end, we will all share the same victory in Heaven.

But that doesn't mean we are the same in every way. That doesn't mean every player is equally gifted or qualified to play every position on the team.

Discussion Question: Have you ever had to play a new position on a team that you had never played before, or been forced to play a sport that you didn't enjoy? What was that experience like?

You may be an amazing sprinter, but that doesn't mean you are also good at throwing the discus. You may be a great pitcher on your softball team, but that doesn't mean the coach expects you to play outfield too. For the same reasons, God does not expect everyone in the church to all fill the same roles. God made us differently and gifted us differently, and those differences bring strength to both a team and a church.

You are a part of the Body

Through the Holy Spirit, God gives all of us something that we can contribute to the church. We all have a role to fill in the church, just like your body is made up of many parts that all serve a unique function.

Romans 12:4-5 (NIV1984)

[4] Just as each of us has one body with many members, and these members do not all have the same function, [5] so in Christ we who are many form one body, and each member belongs to all the others.

If you think about how your body works, you can figure out how you are to play a part in the church. Every body part exists for the good of the body. It is meant to contribute to the health of the whole body. In the same way, you have something – a talent, a gift, an ability – that will benefit the church.

1 Corinthians 12:14-18 (NIV)

[14] Now the body is not made up of one part but of many. [15] If the foot should say, "Because I am not a hand, I do not belong to the body," it would not for that reason cease to be part of the body. [16] And if the ear should say, "Because I am not an eye, I do not belong to the body," it would not for that reason cease to be part of the body.

[17] If the whole body were an eye, where would the sense of hearing be? If the whole body were an ear, where would the sense of smell be? [18] But in fact God has arranged the parts in the body, every one of them, just as he wanted them to be.

You are where you are for a reason. God placed you in your church with a purpose, a unique gift or contribution to make for the common good of that body. He formed you in a certain way, and that includes your age, your talents, your resources, your friendships, your experiences, and even your weaknesses and failures.

1 Corinthians 12:21-22 (HCSB)

[21] So the eye cannot say to the hand, "I don't need you!" Or again, the head can't say to the feet, "I don't need you!" [22] But even more, those parts of the body that seem to be weaker are necessary.

Paul mentions the "weaker" parts of the body for two reasons. One is that you may think that you don't have much to offer, or that you can do much that counts for your church, and that is simply not so. That last verse assures us that every part – every Christian in the church – is necessary.

Secondly, if that verse wasn't there, then you might be afraid to share your struggles or failures or weaknesses with others in the church. But our physical bodies don't work like that. The parts of our body protect and compensate for each other. If one part is hurting, it sends signals through the nervous system to let the rest of the body know it needs help. It's the same with the church. Christ established the church as one more way of helping and supporting you. There are people there who have been through what you are going through. There are wise, more mature disciples there who can help you with your questions and when you are feeling weak or discouraged.

We all have weaknesses that require us to depend on other parts of the body for healing or protection.

1 Corinthians 12:26 (HCSB)

[26] So if one member suffers, all the members suffer with it; if one member is honored, all the members rejoice with it.

The church, despite its problems, is the healthiest place you can be. Connected to that body is where you find help and also a purpose. You are being connected to a body that is supposed to be dedicated to each other.

Galatians 6:1-2 (NLT)
Dear brothers and sisters, if another believer is overcome by some sin, you who are godly should gently and humbly help that person back onto the right path. And be careful not to fall into the same temptation yourself. [2] Share each other's burdens, and in this way obey the law of Christ.

Discussion Question: Describe some ways you have seen others use their talents or gifts for Christ (remember that may not be on Sunday morning or even in the church building). Although you may not yet know, are there some ways you sense you would be best used for Christ and his church? Do you have a sense of your spiritual gifts?

- Read Romans 12:5-8 for examples of spiritual gifts.

Welcome to the Family!

Another common analogy for the church is the family. Sometimes the church is called a family; sometimes it is called the "household of God."

Galatians 6:10 (NLT)
[10] Therefore, whenever we have the opportunity, we should do good to everyone—especially to those in the family of faith.

1 Timothy 3:14-15 (NIV)
I am writing you these instructions so that, if I am delayed, you will know how people ought to conduct themselves in God's household, which is the church of the living God, the pillar and foundation of the truth.

The Church is a household or family belonging to God the Father. Just like any family, there are difficulties, and we have to figure out how to get along. No church is perfect. You have probably already seen disagreements in your church. There are probably some people there who have disappointed you, and who are not as spiritually mature as they should be. There are people there who are difficult to like.

That brings up something important about the church family, and it's true about our biological families, too: You don't have to *like* everyone in your church family, but you must *love* them.

We don't always like every person in our own families, but we do for family because we love them. And just like in your family, there will be some members of your church family who are going through an awkward stage, and some are immature right now, and some are hurting and bitter. We're not all going to like each other for all sorts of reasons, and that's okay. We are not commanded to like each other. That is not what families are for. Families are the place where we honestly love each other.

To remind us of that family bond, of that deeper love that unites us despite our differences, Jesus commanded us to do something together that every family does – share a meal. Just like your family gathers for meals, especially during holidays, the church family gathers to share a meal every Sunday. It's a symbolic meal called communion.

1 Corinthians 10:16-17 (NASB95)
Is not the cup of blessing which we bless a sharing in the blood of Christ? Is not the bread which we break a sharing in the body of Christ? Since there is one bread, we who are many are one body; for we all partake of the one bread.

After you are baptized, you will start sharing in that symbolic meal. Communion is richly symbolic of many things, but remember, every time you take it, that you are taking it with the family that Christ gave to you. Remember that you must love them because of how Christ loved you. You can forgive them because Christ forgave you.

So here is what we have learned about the church:

Baptism joins us to Christ and the Church. The church is essential to us as disciples, and we are essential to the church. God has placed us in the church with unique gifts and opportunities for a purpose. The church is also like a new family for us, to support and guide us as we grow up spiritually. You don't have to like everyone in the church, but you must love them. Communion is a symbolic meal that brings our church family together to remind us that we are to love and forgive each other as Christ love and forgave us.

#6 QUESTIONS
how we baptize and why

This chapter is a collection of questions about baptism and some of the ways people may disagree about baptism. These questions may not be questions for you at all, but it will still be helpful for you to understand these doctrinal issues.

Is there a difference if I am baptized by sprinkling or immersion?

Baptism should be understood as immersion, not sprinkling. *Baptize* is a transliteration of the Greek word *baptizō,* which meant "to immerse." It was also used to convey the idea of sinking or even of drowning. The general usage expressed the idea of going under or perishing. [*Vol. 1*: *Theological dictionary of the New Testament.* 1964- (G. Kittel, G. W. Bromiley & G. Friedrich, Ed.) (electronic ed.) (530). Grand Rapids, MI: Eerdmans.]

The practice of the early Christians was immersion under water. Only years later did some people start to substitute the practice of sprinkling, and that was originally intended as a measure of expediency.

To be obedient to the meaning of the word, to the original practice, and to the symbolism of being "buried with Christ in baptism" (Romans 6:4), you need to be immersed. Baptism is a pantomime of the death, burial, and resurrection of Christ, which we unite to in baptism. The problem with sprinkling is that you didn't bury anything. It ignores both the meaning of the word and the meaning of the act.

What about "accept Jesus into your heart"? Is that the same as baptism, or can I do that instead of baptism?

Some churches teach that to be saved and forgiven, you just need to "accept Jesus into your heart" and say a prayer, usually called "The Sinner's Prayer." Those churches may also baptize people, but they probably teach that baptism is a sign of being saved, and not when you are saved.

The problem with that teaching is that the phrase "accept Jesus into your heart" appears nowhere in the Bible. A "Sinner's Prayer" is also nowhere in the Bible. Not once in the New Testament are people told to say a prayer and accept Jesus into their hearts. That practice is fairly common in churches today, but it is not true to what was taught and practiced by the first Christians. Here is the consistent teaching of the apostles about how to be obedient to the gospel:

Acts 2:37-38 (ESV)
[37] *Now when they heard this they were cut to the heart, and said to Peter and the rest of the apostles, "Brothers, what shall we do?"* [38] *And Peter said to them, "Repent and be baptized every one of you in the name of Jesus Christ for the forgiveness of your sins, and you will receive the gift of the Holy Spirit.*

Do I have to be baptized in a church in front of a crowd?

The simple answer to that is no. You can be baptized anywhere, at any time, publicly or privately. The best example of that is when Philip baptized a man (often called the Ethiopian Eunuch) while they were talking together while riding in a chariot.

Acts 8:36 (ESV)
[36] And as they were going along the road they came to some water, and the eunuch said, "See, here is water! What prevents me from being baptized?"

What prevents me? Nothing! It doesn't require a church building. It doesn't have to happen on a Sunday. The eunuch was baptized in a pond on the side of a road, with no one but Philip and the people traveling with him. You may want to go to somewhere – a campground, a waterfall, a beach, a river – that has special meaning to you.

It is understandable if you have some hesitation about doing this in front of a lot of people, especially if you go to a large church. But think about it: In baptism you are joining Christ's church. You will need those people in the coming weeks, months and years. You are dedicating yourself to serving and loving them, and they have declared the same towards you, so why prevent them from sharing in this? You are going to spend all eternity with them anyway. You are not being baptized to hide anything. It is certainly not something to be ashamed of, but to celebrate.

What if I was already baptized as an infant? Do I have to be baptized again?

Acts 8:12 (NIV1984)

[12] But when they believed Philip as he preached the good news of the kingdom of God and the name of Jesus Christ, they were baptized, both men and women.

Belief is what prompts baptism. To believe, you must understand what you are doing, and you must be able to choose to be obedient. An infant baptized by his or her parents does not understand, cannot yet believe, and is not doing so as a personal choice.

If you were baptized as an infant, you can be thankful that you had parents who cared about your spiritual future, but infant baptism is not an accurate understanding of what the scriptures teach about baptism. If you were baptized as a baby, then yes, you do need to be baptized again, but when you understand what you are doing, and when you are ready to repent and make the commitment of baptism based on your belief, not what someone is doing to you.

Are there situations where someone can or should be re-immersed?

Some people were baptized when they were very young, and later in life feel that they did not understand well enough what they were doing. Other people were baptized as part of a certain denomination and then later start attending a different church and feel like they have a better understanding of baptism and want to do again with more confidence in their understanding of what they are doing.

There is a story in the Bible about being baptized a second time.

Acts 19:2-5 (ESV)
[2] And he said to them, "Did you receive the Holy Spirit when you believed?" And they said, "No, we have not even heard that there is a Holy Spirit." [3] And he said, "Into what then were you baptized?" They said, "Into John's baptism." [4] And Paul said, "John baptized with the baptism of repentance, telling the people to believe in the one who was to come after him, that is, Jesus." [5] On hearing this, they were baptized in the name of the Lord Jesus.

In this instance, Paul baptized these disciples again because their earlier baptism was based on an incomplete understanding of Christ. So yes, there is a precedent for being baptized again if you feel you did not understand well enough or if your heart was not right when you were previously baptized.

If you are struggling with that question, ask yourself where it is coming from. If it is because you are feeling guilty about wandering away spiritually or some moral failure, that doesn't require a re-commitment through baptism. You may need to pray for forgiveness and repentance, reconnect with the Holy Spirit, or make amends with some people you have wronged, but you don't have to "die again" in baptism for forgiveness. Forgiveness is already available to you because of your baptism.

If you were baptized at an age that you now think was too young, you no doubt have matured since then, and you are more knowledgeable of scripture and life since then, but that doesn't require re-immersion either. We will all hopefully continue to advance in spiritual maturity as we age. If you responded in faith to what you knew of the gospel when you were baptized, God accepts that and His grace is sufficient for the gaps that existed in our understanding.

If you are not at peace with your first baptism, here are the questions that may be most important: Were you immersed based on your own belief, your own repentance, and your own commitment? If you were not, if you were baptized more to please someone else, or if your motivation was more about acceptance than repentance, then perhaps you should be immersed again for your own piece of mind.

Biblical examples such as the Philippian jailer in Acts 16 don't give us much background on what a convert knew beforehand, but it is clear that not every disciple went through a 6-week class or was given a checklist before being baptized. Baptism should be an informed decision, but grace is sufficient for what is initially lacking between one's belief and one's knowledge.

[Having said that, if someone is not at peace and has doubts or regrets about his/her first baptism, I usually agree to immerse them again. That's my personal stance, but not every minister or teacher would agree.]

Is baptism an "outward sign" of faith, but not really necessary?

Nowhere in the New Testament is baptism described as an outward sign. Just like the phrase "accept Jesus into your heart," this is another phrase that is often heard but appears nowhere in the scriptures. Those that teach this usually cite this scripture:

Romans 10:9-10, 13 (ESV)
9 because, if you confess with your mouth that Jesus is Lord and believe in your heart that God raised him from the dead, you will be saved. 10 For with the heart one believes and is justified, and with the mouth one confesses and is saved. 13 For "everyone who calls on the name of the Lord will be saved."

They say that clearly here belief is what saves you and baptism isn't even mentioned. Yes, but in that verse, Paul is quoting from Joel 2:32, which says, "everyone who calls on the name of the Lord shall be saved."

That same verse from Joel was quoted by Peter in his sermon on the Day of Pentecost, and Peter ended that sermon telling the crowd "Repent and be baptized, every one of you, in the name of Christ." To Peter, that scripture obviously did not erase the need for baptism.

It didn't erase it for Paul either. Look at what he wrote just two chapters earlier in the same letter:

Romans 6:3-4 (ESV)
3 Do you not know that all of us who have been baptized into Christ Jesus were baptized into his death? 4 We were buried therefore with him by baptism into death, in order that, just as Christ was raised from the dead by the glory of the Father, we too might walk in newness of life.

Our connection to Christ's death is by baptism. And that is "in order that" we too might connect to Christ's resurrection. Baptism creates a necessary connection.

Now some people have an issue with that because they feel that makes baptism a work, a ritual through which we *earn* salvation. They point to scriptures like this:

Ephesians 2:8-9 (ESV)
8 For by grace you have been saved through faith. And this is not your own doing; it is the gift of God, 9 not a result of works, so that no one may boast.

But if you look at how that word *works* is used elsewhere in the New Testament, it's talking about feeding and clothing the poor, it's talking about the fruit of the Spirit. To call baptism a "work" doesn't fit the context of this scripture or the concept of works in general.

When people try to discount the importance or necessity of baptism, and diminish it within the process of salvation, what are they fighting against? Baptism is not difficult. This is not asking a lot of us. And the precedent is unmistakable in the New Testament. Look at what each of these people did when they became disciples of Jesus:

Paul in Acts 9:18 *Then he got up and was baptized.*

Cornelius in Acts 10:48 *And he commanded them to be baptized in the name of Jesus Christ.*

Lydia in Acts 16:15 *And after she was baptized . . .*

Philippian Jailer in Acts 16:30-33 *and he was baptized at once, he and all his family.*

The Bereans in Acts 17:10-12 (NIV1984) [10] *As soon as it was night, the brothers sent Paul and Silas away to Berea. On arriving there, they went to the Jewish synagogue.* [11] *Now the Bereans were of more noble character than the Thessalonians, for they received the message with great eagerness and examined the Scriptures every day to see if what Paul said was true.* [12] *Many of the Jews believed, as did also a number of prominent Greek women and many Greek men.*

Now it is true that it says the Bereans believed, but doesn't say they were baptized. But look at the precedent in Acts: every individual conversion account in Acts includes baptism. Based on that, what do you think Paul and Silas instructed the Bereans to do when they believed?

And look at the very next story of conversion in Acts:

Acts 18:8 (HCSB)
[8] *Crispus, the leader of the synagogue, believed the Lord, along with his whole household. Many of the Corinthians, when they heard, believed and were baptized.*

It doesn't say that Crispus was baptized, but the next sentence implies that all those who believed were baptized, which would include Crispus.

Based on the consistent emphasis in doctrine and practice in scripture, there is no useful reason or even biblical way to argue that salvation happens at some point in a process before baptism or without baptism. Baptism is simply what we do in obedience when we believe.

What will God do with people who believe but are not or cannot be immersed?

The classic example is the criminal on the cross. Jesus tells him "today you will be with me in Paradise," and soon after Jesus dies and that criminal dies, and obviously that criminal was not baptized after appealing to Jesus. He died right there.

Or what about a person who comes to belief in a hospital bed, but because of his medical condition, it is physically impossible to emerge him underwater? What about if he dies unbaptized?

Or you may hear the hypothetical of someone who believes and repents, but on the way to the church to be baptized, he is hit by a train or something. What happens to an unbaptized person like that?

John 3:18 (NLT)
There is no judgment against anyone who believes in him. But anyone who does not believe in him has already been judged for not believing in God's one and only Son.

In the unlikely scenario that someone believes and repents but is prevented from baptism, "there is no judgment" against them. Belief for most of us would lead to baptism, but in the rare case where someone believes but cannot get baptized, this verse says that God will accept their belief.

It simply comes down to this: God ultimately judges every one of us, and he can forgive and save whomever he wants to. He knew the heart of that criminal on the cross, and he forgave him as the true and perfect righteous judge that he is. He knows all of our hearts, and our circumstances, and what we could or could not do. We can trust that God is the perfect judge who always judges rightly.

We can leave those complicated scenarios to the righteous God. All we can do is be responsible for ourselves, and know that after his resurrection, Jesus commanded his followers to make disciples by baptizing them, and every convert after that command is baptized, and the apostles clearly link belief and baptism. With all that, there is no good reason to question the necessity of baptism. Wouldn't you rather just be obedient and be baptized?

ABOUT THE AUTHOR

Scott Franks has served in various ministry capacities for churches in Texas, Oklahoma, and Georgia. Other books and curriculum by Scott can be found at **www.scottgarret.com**. He is also a contributor to *728b* and *Leading Churches.*

Made in the USA
Columbia, SC
14 February 2023